RED OCHER

Miller Williams Poetry Series
EDITED BY PATRICIA SMITH

RED OCHER

Jessica Poli

The University of Arkansas Press
Fayetteville
2023

Copyright © 2023 by The University of Arkansas Press. All rights reserved.
No part of this book should be used or reproduced in any manner without
prior permission in writing from the University of Arkansas Press or as
expressly permitted by law.

ISBN: 978-1-68226-229-0
eISBN: 978-1-61075-794-2

27 26 25 24 23   5 4 3 2 1

Manufactured in the United States of America

Designed by Liz Lester
Cover image: "Fading Song" by Tiffany Bozic
Cover design: Charlie Shields

♾ The paper used in this publication meets the minimum requirements
of the American National Standard for Permanence of Paper for
Printed Library Materials Z39.48-1984.

Library of Congress Cataloging-in-Publication Data

Names: Poli, Jessica, author.
Title: Red ocher / Jessica Poli.
Description: Fayetteville: The University of Arkansas Press, 2023. |
   Series: Miller Williams poetry series | Summary: "In Jessica Poli's Red
   Ocher, the wild mortality of the natural world merges with melancholic
   expressions of romantic loss: a lamb runt dies in the night, a first-time
   lover inflicts casual cruelties, brussels sprouts rot in a field, love goes
   quietly and unbearably unrequited. This is an ecopoetics that explores
   the cyclical natures of love, desire, and grief"—Provided by publisher.
Identifiers: LCCN 2022040579 (print) | LCCN 2022040580 (ebook) |
   ISBN 9781682262290 (paperback) | ISBN 9781610757942 (ebook)
Classification: LCC PS3616.O56455 R44 2023 (print) | LCC PS3616.O56455
   (ebook) | DDC 811/.6—dc23/eng/20221014
LC record available at https://lccn.loc.gov/2022040579
LC ebook record available at https://lccn.loc.gov/2022040580

Supported by the Miller and Lucinda Williams Poetry Fund

CONTENTS

So you'd think, in the second year of my three-year term as Miller Williams Poetry Prize series editor, that I've clicked into a rhythm, undaunted by the hundreds of spectacular submissions flooding my inbox, and reliant on my stellar crew of screeners—all schooled in my exacting standards—to sift through all the goodness and present me with fifty stunners, from which I pluck the three clear winners, each one having risen to the top of the pile with the relentlessness of a north star.

Whew. *That* is overwritten.

But really—I'm not sure how folks picture this task, but it is, in turns, mystifying, exhilarating, and utterly impossible.

At the very heart of the difficulty is that age-old question, *What makes a good poem?* I have been confronted with that pesky query hundreds of times—served up by grade-schoolers, bookstore patrons, confounded undergrads, reading groups, festivalgoers, workshop participants, curious onlookers, byliners and bystanders, and folks just looking to make conversation when I tell them what I do. (And no—it's not just you—it took a *long* time before I was able to state "I am a poet" without tacking on something that felt legitimizing and more jobby, like ". . . oh, and a greeter at Walmart.")

What makes a good poem depends very much on who's doing the reading, when they're doing the reading, and issues and insight they brought to the table before starting to read. It's insanely subjective. At the beginning of my appointment as series editor (I almost said "at the beginning of my reign"—must be the scepter Billy Collins passed down to me), I was asked what kind of poems constituted the books I'd be looking for. Here's what I said:

> I love poems that vivify and disturb. No matter what genre we write in, we're all essentially storytellers—but it's poets who toil most industriously, telling huge unwieldy stories within tight and gorgeously controlled confines, stories that are structurally and sonically adventurous, and it's magic every time it happens. Simply put, when I read a poetry book, I want something to shift in my chest. I want my world to change.

That obviously was one bridge too far for a few folks, who wailed on social media—the primary forum for wailing—that my standards were merely unattainable. One incensed Tweeter (or is it "Tweeterer"?) was particularly riled by the "shift in my chest / world change" thing.

Who in their right mind believes that poetry can actually change the world? THIS world? Why are we teaching our younguns such lofty dribble? Why should the average poet submit a manuscript with absolutely no chance of shifting anything in this strange woman's chest? Alas, come down from that mountain, Madam Editor—can mere mortals get a break?

I want to repeat—and clarify—that good poetry should not leave you the same as when you came to it. I see that as a relatively simple ask on the part of the poet:

> *I have a story. It's a familiar story, but I'm going to tell it in a way you haven't heard before. I want to give the story to you. Take it with you. Live it.*
> *Now my story is part of your story.*

You'd be amazed at how many things I've felt that way about. The way Boo screeches "Kitty!" at the end of the film *Monsters, Inc.* A hard-rhymed scrawl by a sixth grader at Lillie C. Evans Elementary School in the Liberty City section of Miami. A poem written by a student of mine at Princeton—structured like an application form, it morphed into a heartbreaking and revealing piece about his being embarrassed by his aging mother. The children's book *Don't Let the Pigeon Ride the Bus!.* Everything ever penned by Gwendolyn Brooks. The one and only poem written by a reticent mumbler in my Staten Island Intro to Creative Writing class, because it was his one and only poem and he said he'd never write a poem at all. "Antarctica Considers Her Explorers" by Diane Ackerman. The song "Ooo Baby Baby" as crooned by one Smokey Robinson.

I say all that to say this: I am moved by many things, none of them perfection. None of them haughty or precise or manipulative. None of them professional or studied or "officially sanctioned" in any way. I seldom know what I need until it has arrived. I do know that that shift in my chest, that rock to my world, can come from anywhere—somewhere simple, somewhere complex. Anywhere a moment, a voice, a song, or a poem reaches out and finds someone.

I can assure you that the three winners of this year's Miller Williams series are all—I've checked—mere mortals. Each one took a different road to reach me; each one changed my world in a different way. There is no one voice, and there is no one way to hear a voice.

Let's look at the winners, from third to first, from runners-up to crown, Miss America style.

Red Ocher by Jessica Poli is a lush collision of aubade, cento and ghazal, poems that snug cozily into forms that were born waiting for them, poems that pulse outward from a relentless core of sensuality and heartbreak to embody what nature does to us. I am wholly envious of Jessica, because I find such concise lyricism to be difficult to manage. And having grown up surrounded by concrete and hard edges where pigeons were the only wildlife, I can't help but be mesmerized by a poem like "The Morning After"—

> When I opened the door to the coop
> and saw three chickens and a mallard lying dead
>
> in the soggy pine chips, I thought the raccoon
> had made clean kills of all the birds it wanted
>
> in the night. So forgive me if I shouted
> when I walked into the yard and saw the duck
>
> standing motionless, head covered in blood,
> a marble statue after a war.

What's stamped on me, what follows me into my dreaming, is the instance after, the necessary sacrifice of the dying duck, who flees, headless, "before it stopped / and sank to the ground where its neck arced / and swung, mourning itself."

What I'm changed by is the breath I hold in from the beginning of the title poem "Red Ocher":

> To paint the barn bloody.
>
> After all that planting, the peppers rot off the vine.
>
> Wind was once oil. Soil has memories.
>
> What's lost in the retelling.
>
> To fall apart or believe.
>
> The farmer, filling the wheelbarrow with sawdust, remembering last
>   year's weather: *That was a different God.*
>
> What the wasp dragging its half-severed tail knows about sorrow.

Jessica teaches a softer violence, the tender face of it. Her deftly crafted stanzas, her mastery of form, her lean uncluttered way of nudging us forward—all those things make *Red Ocher* a book that undeniably deserves the accolades coming its way.

Up next—well hello there, Ms. L. J. Sysko! You are a wildness and a weirdness, and I would like to play a role in unleashing you upon the world. Your book, *The Daughter of Man*, is gleeful and quicksilver, not willing to sit still for categorization. I'm *here* for it.

L. J. is the risk-taker, the unveiler, the irreverent namer of things. Witness "Trompe L'Oeil," a disrespectful ode to a former teacher:

> Like a kid climbing through the window: eyes wide, shirt billowing open with the heat of hijinks, I'm back—grabbing you by the Peter Pan collar to chew gum in your class, drop your hall pass in the toilet, and eat your breakfast for lunch. I won't recover my manners, no, they're pinned up there under the postcards, ribboned fast to a bulletin board between lion and lamb. You sat the girls in the back of the class and taught math to the front. And I guess I have the option of being less mad, but my upset's been tipping on the precipice forever, like a Medici cherub poised for a rotunda-fall.

Let's take a wee tour of L. J.'s mind, shall we? Up next, from the poem "I may":

> If I want, I may ultrasound each month to monitor
> hornets' nest activity. I may bushwhack to witness
>   watering-hole power dynamics. If I want, I may
> write ethnographies about cultural reciprocity
>   or muse at the wisdom of using blood as currency.
> It's my vagina/uterus/cervix, so you can't tell me
>   I haven't wasted whole days microscope-hunched,
> waiting for something to happen.
>   Days wishing happenings would stop.

Who can stop there? See more of what I saw:

What's stupid

> is, even if aliens do
> mean us harm and descend

the way they did in comic books—
all jumbo-almond eyes, peach-pit heads,
and pistachio-ice-cream skin,
knocking the totem off Bob's Big Boy roof,
even if they utter language that's frozen and vegetable,
even if, with weapons drawn or peace in our puny hearts,
we're vaporized, liquefied, or harvested as fuel—I'll still feel
the jubilant force of epiphany. The way a pearl peering out
of a knife-pried oyster might behold a kitchen.
The way a woman dwelling within a paneled parlor
might put the phone receiver down,
return to preparing dinner, folding laundry,
Gunsmoke or *Green Acres*,
having just heard
the unutterable word.

The Daughter of Man is gleefully unapologetic, upending the familiar and blasting it with motion, heat, and consequence. It's a wide-eyed stroll through the real world, reintroducing me to moments I just might remember living—moments made new with liberal dashes of L. J.'s humor and singular insight.

This year's Miller Williams Poetry Prize top choice, *To Be Named Something Else* by Shaina Phenix, absolutely refuses to behave on the page. Something shifted in my chest with the book's very first poem, because I know—actually, was one of—those blue-black summer girls waiting for some bad boys to twist open the fire hydrant and cool us off:

> See us,   summered in waters most definitely troubled,   stubborn &
>   never
> actually putting any fires out,   rinsing our summertime heavies down
>   into the sewers.
> Little Black   so & so's   walk through water   like we Moses or
>   something.
> See her, all copper & running over   like she God, a cup,   or
>   something.

With "Hydrant Ode," and with so many of the other poems that make up this electric collection, Shaina enlivens the everyday—the everyday miraculous, the everyday hallelujah, the numbing everyday love, the everyday risk of just being Black and living.

There is absolutely nowhere these poems aren't—we're dancing and sweating through our clothes, terminating a pregnancy in a chilled room of white and silver, finally gettin' those brows threaded and nails did, practicing gettin' the Holy Ghost, sending folks to their rest, having babies, listening carefully to the lessons of elders, and sometimes even talking back.

In the brilliant "La Femme Noire: A Choreopoem," a piece in conversation with Ntozake Shange's *For Colored Girls Who Have Considered Suicide / When the Rainbow Is Enuf*, a young Black girl ("perhaps myself," Shaina suggests) queries the elders in an attempt to pull them closer:

> *Who are you and whom do you love?*
>
> *What do you remember about blood?*
>
> *Who is responsible for the suffering of your mother?*
>
> *Tell me something you've never said to your body.*

Of course, I did what all the fortunate readers of this book will inevitably do. I walked into the poem and answered every question for myself. And with my answers, I found new pathways, new ways to be drawn into Shaina's work.

To Be Named Something Else is a book of reason and reckoning, substance and shadow. It's tender and wide-aloud and just about everything we need right now, when both reason and reckoning are in such woefully short supply. And Shaina's superlative combination of formalism and funk consistently astounds— deftly crafted ghazals, sonnets, the pantoum, the duplex, the sestina, and other usta-be traditional structures (I say "usta-be" because they are hereafter transformed) are all on display here.

And not simply on display. They come to conquer.

Every page is stamped with a defiant signature—in fact, I guarantee there's no way you can flip past "Shug Avery Identifies as Pansexual, Poly, and Dares You to Say Anything about It," "The Burning Haibun Remembers Who I Am," or "American Pantoum with Bullet-Holes & Wall." Shaina Phenix will pull in you, and she will hold you there. And, by God, you won't want to move.

I leave you with a stanza from "Sermon," one that resounds with me, if any one stanza can be said to typify the power of this collection:

Mother god in the name of Girl   I come to you
as alive as I know how asking you to be
an unbloodied knuckle sandwich, be unfucked, and in
an undulant ocean of selves and salt bone of my befores. Be the first word
out of my mother's reborn mouth. Be swine-repellent or the pearls that
    look
like pearls but don't bust from too much pressing   down. Be that
which is holy and make dogs deathly allergic. Be
me in an un-rendable skin-sheet. Let this poem (Earth? Body?) ? Be all
    of you
and none of me for the sake of your people.   Amen.

—*Patricia Smith*

I

It's morning, and in my arms
another lamb is dying.

I've done this before.
Watched a horse, bloated

and belly-up, jerk its legs in its stall
before the vet came with her needle

to soothe it. But here,
this small shaking body

seems like a bigger death—
her short breath on my neck,

the stain of yellow-green shit
soaking the center of my shirt

from where her back legs press.
Maybe I'm making too much

of the way her eyes close
as she finishes the bottle of milk,

how her head falls against my chest
as if to say: I trust you

as much as one animal can trust another.
If love were ingestible, wouldn't it

take the form of milk
warm from a mother's teat?

This milk is from a goat, but the lamb
would never know, being the runt

of the litter, kicked away
by her own mother's sharp hoof.

With what tangible vessel of love
can I nurse her?

And here I'll admit that, in my head,
I'm already writing this poem—have already

arrived at the image of the shit
blooming on my shirt like a flower

or a patch of green lichen.
And I've looked at her throat

and thought about how I would cut it
if I had to, if her suffering

grew larger than what her body
could contain; have watched videos

on how to do it;
and now, holding her,

I picture bright droplets of blood
scattered on the pine chips below us,

and I know—I'm ashamed to say it—
that it would be beautiful.

Aubade with Benediction

I remember sun and sweet corn
by the acre. Sorghum swaying

like a backwards broom. The bindweed
spreading, crabgrass slinking

through the cabbage.
Days that felt suspended—the fog

erasing the silo, the air quiet
like a woman praying.

Behind the barn, a basin
catching rain and chore light.

Rabbits in the onion field.
Tomatoes glowing lamplike.

Heirloom seeds in a sun-warm fist;
the field in flower. Field like

falling. Field with broken
shadow. Field inside of

body. Body as in holy.
As in what comes after.

Night wears your sweat
like an antlered buck

carrying moss.
Another wineglass breaks,

accidentally tapped
against the kitchen faucet.

Out in the dark,
a goat is bleating—

a milkstone lodged
in her udder.

The night flees on hooves.

Forest Cento

What were we meant to find?
When your hand is on my knee

like a crooked arrow
dragging itself through the dark,

what can I offer?
I slip your hand under my skirt

to greenery. —The brief moment
mosses. What heat is this in me

cracking to bend an arrow
again,

again,
again?

Sudden switches
    in direction and weather.

Bends in the road
    come as scythes:

falciform, sharpened.
    As light ebbs,

hawks loop.
    Needly pines

pin themselves to the sky.
    Farmlands rise, fall—

barns half-eaten
    in the dark.

The Barn

I go there now, walk on molding feathers,
           dead hen in the corner. Where we held sweaty hands
      and pushed together foreheads. The room where I

undressed, where beside sacks of flour
           and creased Bible pages I curled my new
      and unused body around yours. Here,

I shed a teaspoon of blood
           while you peeled me like the rind
      of an unripe fruit, gnats and barn flies

working their way between our torsos.
           I know now that things die.
      A rotting hen told me. She said, from the corner

of the room: *You know you'll have to start over.*
           The barn door's deadbolt still isn't thrown
      (my fingers too sore, too stiff) but it won't matter,

you'll never try to get in again. The barn will stay quiet
           and continue to rot, and I will remember the mold
      growing on that hen as I stand in a hot steaming room,

in light that comes through stacks of dirty dishes,
           and I'll remove pieces of myself to boil in cloudy water
      and add spine, vertebrae: scraps for a new body

drawn up over breakfast including a detailed map
           of every artery and vein and every inch of my skin
      that wouldn't have been touched by you.

I drink until my eyes
fog with you,
my first lover,

who told me
I was an unopened
root system.

I wanted, for a long time, to be anything
wildgood
by which I mean

what no other can know.
Blood memory:
it felt like a barn

opening
in my two hands.
The endless ground under us.

I'm that person who can't stop
asking to be bent, taken by firelight.
I lie here now as I once lay

as in here I am, here I am.

Archival

Now the last things we said are like the moon
on the night we said them: shadow-bound, absent.
An egg tucked in a black cloak, or a form of hunger.
And that moon is like a single run-down house
underneath it: porch bowed and sinking, ill-lit, stale.
Or the handful of straw that I stuffed in your mouth
in my dream last night: dry and tasting of moondust.
And as for the hay rake on the back of the tractor
making neat piles of gold in rows across the field—
that rake and field are like the swelling in my chest
when you called me for the last time and told me,
or might as well have, that the straw in the barn
had been soaked by rain, that out of your mouth, now,
would only come buckets of water instead of moonlight.

I say goodnight from behind
the years it took to kiss me.
Listen to my breathing, your own breathing—
two little animals moon-led,
almost able to feel
we could have anything we wanted.

II

It was simple. Every morning, I opened the barn doors.
I took the pitchfork and the wheelbarrow from their places,

disturbing spiders, sawdust, a hinge of light from a cracked
window which seemed like a sort of memory—a lamp

scraping the dark. Soon the cat would find me, tail swaying,
fat old king on his way to the haystacks for sleep.

The horses eyed me, shifting. Their place was outside,
nostrils flaring, stars falling sharply on their backs.

The history of everything is boundary.
I gave them hay, a hand against their neck. I wish

I'd had more. Some of them, old,
died. I cried for each one.

Unrequited Love Poem

I wake up with the flowers you gave me
in the dream. When it rains like this,
I think of you in the corn. How all year
we read weather like the holy book.

In the dream, when it rains like this,
church bells crawl through the window.
I read weather like the holy book
until night comes on black stilts.

Church bells crawl through the window
and into my body which shudders
until night comes. On black stilts
I walk through the dream

and into my body, which shudders
like a dog left out in the cold.
I walk: through the dream
I find you, hunting through fields

like a dog. Left out in the cold
for too long, you shiver my name when
I find you. Hunting through fields
of corn, we rest periodically.

For too long, you shiver my name. When
light breaks there's a sound like rustling
corn. We rest. The dream
repeats: over and over,

light breaks. A rustling sound:
you, in the corn. All year
the dream repeats. Over and over
you give me flowers, which disappear when I wake.

Transient Cento

I'm in a bed. This man and I,
waiting, waiting,

half out of duty and half in flight.
Sleeping, turning in turn like planets

wheeling and drifting, we
move forward, backward,

breathing, breathing.
I know we can't give each other any more,

being over-fearful,
fixed like telescopes on some

memory
coiled up in the dark.

I don't say anything.
In the silence now,

we look at each other and
light trembles years behind us.

I've been down a road once that led to a river that led to a stream that led
to an open field where the horizon was only broken by a single house

and since then I've been lost in thinking about it—the caved-in roof,
porch sagging, owners long dead, silent husk of a house.

I told you about it once, and you told me about the summer you spent
baling hay while the girl you liked watched from her house:

porch swing swaying back and forth, yellow hair, a dog at her feet. I wonder
if you ever saw me like that—a moment of breath in the heat, a house

for your heart. Months, now, since that night when I was drunk and hopeful
on your couch, sweating, A/C broken, while rain fell outside the house.

You've been quiet since then, and the rain doesn't come
except for brief storm-bursts that batter both our houses.

I haven't told you about the things I've done with my body
since you traced it like a wound in the sky, like a farmhouse

blaring light in the middle of acres of night. How I wished I could unknow you,
and, wishing, spent night after sweat-soaked night in another man's house.

And still I come back to that sagging shack in the field where I found,
for the first time and so long ago, the filament of my desire, housed

in the remnants of another lived life. It would have been nice, I think,
if that had been us—alone in a field, just you, me, a dog, maybe, a house.

The Morning After

When I opened the door to the coop
and saw three chickens and a mallard lying dead

in the soggy pine chips, I thought the raccoon
had made clean kills of all the birds it wanted

in the night. So forgive me if I shouted
when I walked into the yard and saw the duck

standing motionless, head covered in blood,
a marble statue after a war.

And still I'd seen enough death to know
she was near enough to it to be counted

among the ones already scooped into the wheelbarrow.
Even so, I filled the plastic duck pool, hoping

she would splash off her wounds
then go about her day.

But when I placed her in the water
she only bobbed, neck drawn close

against her body where I thought
I glimpsed bone. Sometimes animals tell you

when they're ready. You sharpened
the small ax while I picked her up

and set her on the ground, stretching her neck
across a wooden board, and all the while

she didn't struggle. After the blade came down,
I didn't think to hold her body tightly

and so it leapt from my hands and ran
ten feet before it stopped

and sank to the ground where its neck arced
and swung, mourning itself.

You and I stood over what was left of her.
And yes, we laughed a little afterwards, remembering

the shock of her lunging from my grip,
the way we froze, cartoonlike, at the sight,

but mostly when we talk about it now we grow quiet,
our own memories of the morning filling

the crevasses of our thoughts until a rooster crow
or the bleating of a lamb summons us back.

Picking Mulberries

Here, where only a week ago
the rooster hung with its throat cut,
I spread a tarp
and climb the ladder
to shake branches so the fattest berries
drop like hail.

Gathering them in buckets,
my fingers turn a violent blue.
Sweat drips from the point of my nose,
dotting the tarp. It's been a month

without rain, and the hope of it
starts to wither like the arugula
drooping in the field. Through my shirt

I feel my heart—
the day's heat making it thunder,
pumping blood
the color of my stained hands.

I couldn't fault the moon
for not appearing the night you left.

I could have hidden behind shadow too.

Believe the world is wild but meaningful
and you will spend your nights looking for water where there is none,
sensing weather that won't come.

When you left,
I dreamed a mirror in the sky was burning.
I dreamed the red moon told me how to love.

These stories tell themselves:

a boy walks down the road
and into the woods.

A girl wants to follow
but can't—

wolf-dog biting at her ankles,
one arm tethered to a post in a field.

Knowledge

Not child.
Not straw hair or toy soldiers.
Not walking to the mailbox at the end of the road
with the dog at your heels.
Not, not the green sky.
Not gravy crusted to the pan.
Not the bent wings of birds
or the gnarl of your great-aunt's hands.
Not fearing the attic, its spilled pink insulation.
Not fields. Not frost-covered ground.
Not the biting chill in the hayloft
where you laid yourself down,
aligned your eye with a crack in the floorboard
to watch the stillness of the milking-cow below.
That body, now: not-cow.
Not warm breath or hay-smell, a hand against her flank.
Not to say: memory is a sealed room,
the barn preserved, your eye still molded to wood.
And not to confuse history
with fortune, augured writings on the wall.
Not to marry the barn or to burn it.
Not even to know how.

III

Prothalamion

> A man ought not to marry without having studied anatomy, and
> dissected at least one woman.
>
> —HONORÉ DE BALZAC, *The Physiology of Marriage*

Before the cracked chest   Before
the metal table   Before the cold room

where you go to learn   a woman's soft
and yeasty secrets   do you imagine

inside her body you'll find   cathedral walls
susurrous blood   a sailor's knot

a pomegranate   Do you think it will feel like
a holy act   knowing how often

holiness   shrouds violence
Before you pry her open   will you pray

take tongs and extract   the apple core
wedged   in her lips   Will you

and other men   allemande
around the table   grave and overcome

with ceremony   Will wine be poured
Will you toast   to future brides

their sinews   and yellow bile
Will you discuss   the handkerchiefs you'll give them

embroidered   with strawberries
When you are done   will you cover her with cloth

light cigars   peaty   and dank
Later   will you at odd hours   remember her liver

her spleen   her muscly bladder
Will you   could you   know what it means

I do not want to be a chrysalis again.
I stand on all fours, my fur
like a million flowers on fire—
a newborn animal
not quite earthbroken.
Watching, you
who has never understood me
see how sorrow can
let us be wild and free,
not to forget, but to remember.
Planets howl.
The earth drips through us
like spilt dye from a rock.
Your hands glow like milk in the dark.
I will devour you,
tongue long and purple as an anteater's
and walk a long time in the woods.

Gastronomy

My therapist tells me that the stomach
holds most of our feelings. She doesn't mean
what goes into it, but still I start to dream up
a feast of joy inside my gut. Spinach,
artichokes, oranges slowly peeled in the morning,
lavender tea and honey, cardamom. My list grows
while she leads me through a breathing exercise.
She says *Picture a place where you feel calm,*
and I'm walking down the grocery aisle, past the milk,
pulling a pack of probiotic yogurt off the shelf.
She looks like she eats green smoothies and citrus,
and I think of the lemons molding in my fridge,
turning white and mushy, caving in gently around
one particularly soft crater. What have I fed myself
lately? Olives and oily fish, burnt toast, nervousness,
soup. I ate octopus once at a Greek restaurant
in New York where I drank too much wine
and had to unbutton my jeans after my stomach
swelled over them. My therapist and I don't talk
about my body, except in the sense
that I live in it. Years ago, I ate magic mushrooms
on an empty stomach and three hours later I knew
I was going to die. Even after I didn't, I wasn't
convinced—I thought it was only a matter of time.
I didn't eat for days, afraid I had damaged something
deep inside of me. This, too, I have never told her—
not about the mushrooms, or driving six hours
that week to see my parents because I wanted, secretly,
to say goodbye. Maybe this is what she means
about the stomach. That it holds only
what it's capable of and refuses the rest.

Yesterday I saw a tree the color
of the sky it stood against
and thought of Rothenberg's painting
of the translucent horse
barely outlined in a pink haze—the same color
that lit the glass buildings some mornings

in Pittsburgh, where I studied photography
for one misplaced year. There,
in a darkroom, a girl held my hips
while I mixed chemicals that smelled
like sweat licked off skin,
and the shape of her hands
felt like shadows touching me. I told her

about the horse that lived
at the end of the road where I grew up,
how I fed it handfuls of grass
and dandelions from across
the electric fence. That horse

was a kind of shadow too, forgotten
by the neighbor who asked for it
for her birthday
and then never rode it. Rothenberg's horse

is mid-gallop, legs folded,
body suspended
in pink air. Where is that girl

from the darkroom now? She'd been living
in a tent in the woods when I knew her.
Her arms were covered in red crisscrossed lines.
She told me not to worry about her,
and I, young, didn't. Later, I had dreams

of pink fields, a figure blurring
along the tree line.

They could have left me there
trying clumsily to cover up the stain by myself,
angling my book bag behind me until I made it
to the nurse's wood-paneled office to call my mom
and ask her for a change of clothes.
But they didn't blink—just shuffled me out of that room
and through the halls, parting the crowd like dolphins
in a school of herring, making themselves late for lunch,
or algebra, or gym class where they'd chip their neon nail polish
and spray clouds of Calgon to cover up the warm rubber smell
of dodgeballs and sweat. O girls made of gristle
and glitter, born carrying small funerals in their bellies—
who all knew that one day the evidence might smear itself
across a yellow plastic chair, which a boy might see and forever after
make gagging noises with his friends when she passed by
or entered a room. O girls with their purses full of silver eyeshadow
and tampons, who traded notes through the openings
of lockers, who bought lip-shaped lollipops for each other
on Valentine's Day. I want to kiss the lips now
of every girl who used her body as a shield around mine,
who glared cool eyes at anyone who looked at me,
who, when someone asked why I was wearing different clothes,
told some stunning and beautiful lie
that no one even thought to question.

On Desire

At a strip mine in Pennsylvania,
we were told to lie down
and press our ears to the ground
to feel the blast
ripple by as the miners set off
a charge. When it came,

the dirt rose
against our faces—
a small wave hurrying
through the earth,
a short, chaste kiss.

Greenbrier

Youth Conservation Corps, Laurel Highlands, age 16

That one summer we spent trying to defeat the weeds—
        knocking vines back from trail edges, arms slashed

by thorns, muscles turning gummy from the hedge clipper's tremor
        or the endless pull of a fire rake. There was a boy I liked on the crew

who liked another girl and spent the summer chasing her,
        faked a convincing look of sympathy the day she came in crying,

having finally broken up with her boyfriend of two years.
        Still—they never got together, and I kept up my quiet pining,

noticed how naturally he loped over craggy maintenance trails,
        felt stoned studying his large hands and the way they gripped tools,

only started to name the current that awed through me
        when I thought about those hands in other places.

One morning we hiked three miles to the bottom of Grove Run
        and found a thicket of greenbrier so dense that one of us turned around

and went back for more equipment, the rest falling easily into a choreography
        of cutting and raking, taste of gasoline filling our mouths. As we worked

we spread out, losing sight of one another—far enough, eventually,
        that noise vanished too and the woods

seemed to grow, the thorny plants multiplying, swallowing us whole.
        At lunchtime I threw my rake down and began the slow hike upward,

taking my time, to where we'd dropped our packs. Near the top of the trail,
          I turned around a switchback and saw him:

his body at an angle, leg slightly bent,
               hands held loosely around the root of himself

as he took a piss into the brier he'd been cutting. I backtracked,
               holding my breath behind a knot of maples until he'd finished,

my heart a clatter of hooves, trees falling inside my ears.
               All summer that moment stayed with me while we continued

not falling in love: his stance, the bald frankness of it. The soft of him
               open to the sun. The blush that heated my face

every time I thought of him, of his hands cradled as if praying,
               repenting to the light that poured down, to the glowing sea of green

we'd come there to kill. And afterward, the metallic sound of a zipper
               coming softly through the trees and rocketing into me.

I wanted you to touch me
almost endlessly.
I dreamed as I waited

in the early dark
while my very bones sweated
hunger. Dreamt of snakes

beneath the forest.
My legs open. The air full of water.
If we are made in God's image,

I was as good as I would ever be. In the dark, the ruddy
glow through my breastbone:
some part of me that, almost,

is closer to me than I am to myself.

Afterimage

Mostly I remember the way he laughed
when I tried to kiss him
in the dark field of his bedroom, that place

where I first knew the weight of a body
above mine, the broken ceiling fan over us,
the chair in the corner heaped

with dirty clothes, my black bra
on the floor. That laugh—as if he thought
I was silly for wanting more

than the mechanics of it, the boiled down
sex ed version heard in school halls, a + b =
take off all your clothes, which is what he said

while he searched, naked, for a condom.
Afterwards—I hate this part—he rolled away,
his back to me. I think you know

the rest, that this didn't end
in love, or love's likeness,
but in a phone call

that built a fence between us,
sturdy, the posts weather-treated
and ready for the long winter.

It's while the coffee is brewing
that I start crying again,
thinking of the eggs going bad
in the fridge, the water pipes
frozen, the temperature outside
turning the house into a cage
while across town he has his arm
around some other girl on her birthday.
He never bought me flowers
but there they are on the table
in a picture of the two of them
on Facebook—baby's breath
and carnations, all shades of pink,
two sets of initials drawn sloppily
inside a heart on the front of a card.
I want to eat the flowers stem
by stem and then puke them up—
the mashed petals blooming
in the toilet. My God,
he drew those hearts with his clumsy
hand, stood in a drugstore
picking out just the right card.
I wish I hadn't looked closer, wish
I didn't have to look, wish I'd never
looked his way across a sports-bar
volleyball court to begin with.
I make coffee with water
that's been sitting out for two days
and stare at the screen

where he's smiling, and now the flowers
are really coming up, the floral
fucking hibiscus notes in my coffee
making acid tracks on their way
up my throat, and since the water is still
shut off, I take a gallon from the ones
my landlord left and pour it down
the toilet bowl, watching everything
disappear.

Sorry Cento

I wanted to stay as I was,
pulling arrows out of my heart
so you would not depart, so I would not
for the hundredth hundredth time
stand sullenly in the slowly whitening
nowhere.
Today I sing alone
through a forest of empty armor.
One day after another—
how endless your not-returning,
where I am and am not.

IV

1. Throughout this work, I have found myself
hungry. Eating pieces of myself to sustain myself
as I roamed the forest at the edge of the field.

2. As the fruit ripens, chlorophylls break down to reveal other pigments such as
yellow and red, much like the color change that occurs in some autumn leaves.

3. That same week,
I was looking at the stars
on a back porch far away from the city
where the dark was only punctured
by the neighbor's kitchen light.
Somewhere below, the sheep chewed steadily,
ridding the field of clover
while two coyote packs howled to one another,
a sound which held
the sky and trees together.

4. This leapt out of our discussion about the Horsehead Nebula, which led me to an article explaining that barns are painted red because red paint is cheapest, which is a result of the abundance of iron oxide due to nuclear fusion inside dying stars.

5. grasses moving in the wind

6. Referring to a partial skeleton dyed red, buried in 33,000 BP and discovered in Britain in 1823.

7. The truth is I like to imagine a life like that:
the floors uncluttered, no dirt tracked in,
no muddied socks overflowing the hamper.

8. The line in question read: *Loving you felt like fog seeping into a barn.*

9. Of course, I can't describe the true color. Many have stated that it has lost some of
its intensity over the period of observation.

10. There will be room for desire
again, even after it leaves
like a flood receding,
the damaged farmhouses
and washed-away bridges
lying scattered the next day
amid silt and debris.

11. Here's another attempt to find an open door inside myself.

V

Given that the night and the flesh are cold.
Given that the rope is good and strong
and the tractor starts without choke.

The horse is buried
before first light.

His stall stays empty three days. After which
new sawdust is forked,
a mare led in from the top field.

Weeks go by.
Weather shifts, heaves its weight
against the hedgerow.
The farm rises and falls
like a chest.

One morning
a hawk comes into the barn—
young red-tail, brown spotted belly—and for an hour
he flies back and forth between haystacks
making shadows of the barn lights,
pausing chores in their rhythm of shovel, pitch, shovel
before finding his way again.

Nowhere Cento

In the fields, the silos open their mouths
like dark dark fear.

This is a road where I could die for love
in the laps of farm women.

I want you to walk out into the fields
the way I used to on hot nights,
straight into the crow-cawing dark.

The wild does not have words.
Will you marry it?
It means you cannot go back.

And there was that night in high school
            when Nathan and Jake were in the front seat driving drunk
      and Sarah and I were in the back,

a plastic bottle full of warm orange juice and vodka
            passing between us. It was midnight, maybe later, when we crashed
      through the metal of a stop sign, hitting it once

and then again when it didn't budge. Nathan got out,
            threw the sign in the trunk and kept driving,
      speeding up when we got to a dirt road—

the narrow one behind Sarah's house
            that wound through the dark backwoods like a water snake
      through a creek. Jake said he wanted to ride on the roof

and then he did: facedown and spread-eagle above us,
            whooping and yelling into early autumn night until Nathan
      took a turn too fast

and rammed the car into a bank.
            I remember how Jake's body was briefly lit by the car's headlights
      as he soared toward the trees—   a sudden angel—

blue plaid shirt fanning out and rippling like wings,
            dead leaves like feathers pillowing around him where he landed.
      He got up, brushed dirt off his jeans

and laughed, arms raised: exultant, immortal.
            I was scared, but not enough. At seventeen I didn't know
      how easily a body could break,

had never heard the sound of a mother mourning her son
              and hadn't yet seen the gutted face of a girl my age
     who'd lost her friend the night before

to a car, a frozen lake—his body at the funeral
              swollen from being in the water for so long.
     Nathan died at 22, Jake not long after. Both for the reasons

you might expect. I didn't think about them again until years later when,
              remembering that night, I watched their shapes in the front seat
     abruptly vanish,

leaving a hush of empty space,
              noise from the woods filling the car like a song, like grace,
     like the word *amen.*

To paint the barn bloody.

After all that planting, the peppers rot off the vine.

Wind was once oil. Soil has memories.

What's lost in the retelling.

To fall apart or believe.

The farmer, filling the wheelbarrow with sawdust, remembering last year's
weather: *That was a different God.*

What the wasp dragging its half-severed tail knows about sorrow.

The swollen leg; the rotten tooth.

An iron ore used as pigment.

The man who goes outside to feed the hogs and becomes the meal.

How the sky pulls on a body in pain; in love.

Night, a collapsed star.

Night, a buck's splintered antlers.

Night, stealing the lock from the horse's stall door.

The grief you are born with.

Lord, there's a snake growing out of my chest but I don't claim it.

A battle-bruised skeleton.

The part of the body composed of thunder and faith.

To inherit trauma like a wedding ring.

The storm; the pine shaking; the rope that keeps the boat knocking up against
the dock.

To glance ghost. To taste gun.

To become what you found in the attic when you were young.

Pills barking like young wolves in an empty stomach.

Baling twine choking the straw spreader.

Glissando. Nebula. Blood clot.

To always be crossing: a river, line of salt, graveyard.

The silo collapsing like it was waiting for love that never came.

Burying what's left: of the dog, the bottle, the unsent letter.

A woman walks out the front door, carrying everything.

And the night remembers.

Callused hands against stars.

A bear cub gnawing its own mother's bones.

Did you see the blood in the snow?

The gulls in the parking lot say *yeah, yeah,*
yeah. Something about praying. Something
about stars spinning. The wind coming out
of the trees. The body shuddering like it does.
Taking your hand and holding it like I did
that one night, like I meant to do again.
Now: strike a match and augur what's coming.
Augur the snow falling on the roof, boots
heaped in the mudroom, a bright afternoon,
windows steaming, the last things we said
knocking quietly around inside.

Poem for When You Realize That You'll Never Look at Brussels Sprouts the Same Way Again

When you've spent hours picking them
off their thick stalks thinking he doesn't love you,
will never love you, did he ever even
love you, November weeds wild around you
like you're some kind of frost-summoned half-god-
half-goat, and the cold slices your cracked fingers
and etches the cracks deeper, stinging, drawing blood,
and the white bucket you drag from stalk to stalk
stays mostly empty, the plants bug-eaten
and yielding less each day.
There are many ways of living.
One is with a hole inside of you that never gives
or forgives. Another is to collect memories
as if they're shards of light in what is otherwise pitch-dark.
The buds snap off the stalk like a moose's heavy antlers
shedding in winter. Moments of light:
every slanted balcony in Syracuse. The smell
of brussels sprouts in the oven on Thanksgiving.
Running to fill someone's wineglass in the living room.
Cooking by yourself in your small kitchen in Lincoln,
organic sprouts washed and spread
across the cutting board. Their imperfections—
browned edges, insect tracks. You eat a bowl full of them
and think of people you've loved:
your aunt, a thousand miles away and not speaking to you,
who you want to ask: *When did you first know*
your own sadness? On Friday you go to your therapist's office
and talk about light, about feeling like you're fractured
by light, and she writes and says *yes* and says *okay*

and you drive home in the egg-yolk yellow evening light
and cook dinner. Later, wine-drunk and stoned, you talk
to the ceiling fan and curl your body around the sound of trains
roaring their way into the Nebraskan prairie.
Winter light. Lover's light.
The way light and shadow slanted
across the vegetable field in September, October,
November. The light that glittered in the rainwater
inside the plants' cupped leaves. The light
that fills you now, knowing the things you know,
forgiving yourself the rest.

Red Cento

It will help if you remember
what love is:
only what returns love.
Where are you?
The day is on my tongue, I'm tipsy,
chasing the dead deer.
What love is:
hope, but out of what? what?

Late frost kills off the first
of the daffodils.

Alone in the barn, I find him flat
on the floor of the stall—

belly swollen, sawdust fanned out
in a crater where he'd thrashed.

The moon that morning:
a fingernail drawn

across bedsheets.
So this is life without you,

so this—

VI

The blood from the lamb
wasn't beautiful.

I know this
even not having seen it

(she died in the night)
the same way

it came to me
that the man I loved

would disappear
like a deer flashing

past headlights
into a cornfield.

Later, as I buried her
beside her sisters

on the woody ridge
of the sewage pond,

I recited the names
of the ones who left

shadows in me—
their animal breath

a ghost
in every field I work

where my body still searches
for what it cannot hold.

eating the leftover snow

we speak a shadow-speech

from room to room closing lights

very-stars

rush with a crackling sound over

a lake

and there is so much here

to last us all winter

beauty is this and this and this dull thing

that holds us

in our desolation

I will stay here

like a woman who believes only in the idea

of this life

my heart

pretending to be a thing that opens.

Future History

In the driveway, we look at the moon
through the telescope he carries
from the cobwebbed garage. It's late.
He speaks around a cigarette, narrating
the lunarscape, its mountains and valleys,
while I press my eye to the lens.
He's careful not to touch me
even though only minutes ago
I was wrapped around him—
the darkness of his bedroom
like the sky surrounding the moon.
Afterwards, we look at a nebula,
a streak of red and white dust.
How old is that light, I wonder
but don't ask, because I'm also thinking
of the light between us, trying to pin down
the point at which it will go out.

And here we are now in the place
where the trees flicker on and off.
I came here, climbed the mountain
despite knowing that you didn't want
to be saved. The two of us stand in a circle
of breadcrumbs and broken glass,
a dead horse lashed to my back.
You look at me from your blue mouth.
A lake of gin sloshes behind your eyes.
The horse twitches, and I toe
the ground with my boot. All of us
are coiled, full of green longing.
So that we might find our way down,
we hold out hope for the light.

How to Change

First know that the dark is full of reflections of yourself, all waiting in blackened mirrors. Light a fire as your starting point and then walk backwards, always keeping the flames in sight. When you reach an object, identify it by touch. Take anything useful with you and move on. Once the fire is only a pinpoint of light, stop. This is your new home. Build another fire and then collect the things you've found, separating them into piles according to usefulness. Notice how the air is different here, how your voice sounds slightly changed and you don't yet recognize your hands, which are holding a mirror from the pile of found things. You don't remember taking it, but you know what to do, your new hands somehow already familiar with the motions of burying.

Aubade with Resurrection

When I come to the edge of the wet-dark pasture
in the quiet before the chickens and the neighbor's baby
wake to make noise, I know the lamb is dead.

The runt of triplets, her head had been small enough
that she'd learned to slide it through one of the loose gaps
in the electric fence to reach the clover

on the other side. Now half the fence lies in a heap
where she'd tangled in it, then struggled, choking
while I slept.

Morning dew collects on her brown fur.
Her eyes are two black stones.
I squat in the grass to cradle her still-warm muzzle

and guide her skull back through the fence
while the other sheep watch,
chewing mouthfuls of flowers.

Once free, I wrap my hands around her neck
and carry her, hooves swaying,
to the edge of the pond to be buried.

Just as I reach it, her throat bobs, the suggestion
of a gulp: a muscle reflex, slight ripple under my palm.
In my mind, for a fleeting moment, life returning.

Hunter's Moon

While the sun goes down over the lake,
I can still taste the moon
that we watched last night from the car—
how it hovered, metallic,
over traffic lights and big-box stores.

The geese move slowly across the water.
I'm trying to think about anything
other than the dream I had
after I left you at your house.
In it, the moon was a coin

you placed in my mouth
before pressing your lips against mine.
A killdeer skirts the weeds along the shore—
the first one I've seen in this land-locked state.
The water purples. People

begin leaving, their headlights
falling along the grass where I sit.
Alone, I pull the moon out
from under my tongue
and place it in the grass, an offering.

I'm going to hide behind language
where dead lichens drip
where only present tense survives,
a slow fire
or the shadows' shuddering
through waist-high fields,
which is a memory of my past, which I give to you
in this letter,
as I try to leave you again.

ᴗ

I've lain through animal days.
I think if I speak long enough
inside the belly of the horse,
I won't get blood on the floor.

ᴗ

The horse rears,
the night closes in like water over a stone
and my tongue is split
making a sound like *it is enough that you exist*
while I myself shrink.

ᴗ

I'm trying to say what happened to us

I was a sheaf of wheat
I lay asleep under you
I hollowed myself into a cave
It happened like this, or almost

(here the letter breaks off)

⤵

Maybe you are no one, like the night.

⤵

It's not that I am alone or that you are or why—
we love what we love,
to the bottom. And you,
you can believe me or not.

Holmes Lake

Lincoln, Nebraska

I've forgotten what it feels like to be wanted
the way the Labrador near me wants the stick

his owner throws for him, his body crashing
into the water before pausing, mouth clapped tightly

around the wet bark, to stand turned, awestruck,
toward the setting sun. On the shore, a father

holds his daughter and twirls a piece of long grass
between his fingers as they watch the hills turn glassy

and bright. I sit beneath a tree and watch them all—
dog and owner, man and daughter—and I feel

far away. And it's here that I often see a fisherman
anchored to one particular spot, ice chest and gear

beside him, his blue windbreaker puffed
from air coming off the water as he eats spoonfuls

of beans from a can, pulls hard on a cigarette,
and adjusts his lines. On those days, I wonder

if he wonders what I'm writing the way I wonder
what he does with the fish he catches—who

he shares them with, if anyone, and whether it's him
who picks the bones clean from the flesh, him

who warms the skillet and lays the fish gently
in the crackling oil. Today, though, the girl's mother

stands in the fisherman's usual spot, her phone
poised, snapping a photo every time the light shifts

a little more to darken the clouds gathering
like flies along the fur of the horizon.

I'm reminded of the horse I used to care for
and how, a month before he died, I found him

standing in the round pen behind the barn
with his head raised, eyes turned toward the sun rising

across the valley while the starlings in the hedgerow
gathered in sound before bursting from the trees

all at once, the air suddenly swarming, the horse
tilting his head to watch their departure much like

the Labrador now watches the sun across the lake.
And I knew a dairy farmer once who, when a cow

was to be put down, would turn her out into the pasture
one last time to watch the sun set. I wonder if all

these animals look at the sky and see something
that I never will. I think I could spend

my whole life trying to find it.

"Field of View" references an article by Yonatan Zunger.

Some lines in the poem "Red Ocher" were inspired by the book *Defining the Wind* by Scott Huler.

"Forest Cento" uses lines from Ai, Michael Burkard, H. D., Jorie Graham, Sara Eliza Johnson, Alejandra Pizarnik (translated by Yvette Siegert), and Tomas Tranströmer (translated by Robin Fulton).

"Firelight Cento" uses lines from Leila Chatti, Franny Choi, Robert Creeley, Carolyn Forché, Jorie Graham, Keith Leonard, Sharon Olds, Romeo Oriogun, Alicia Ostriker, Mary Ruefle, Tomas Tranströmer (translated by Robin Fulton), Jean Valentine, and Jane Wong.

"3 A.M. Cento" uses lines from Michael Burkard, Lynn Emanuel, Carolyn Forché, Louise Glück, and Octavio Paz (translated by Muriel Rukeyser).

"Transient Cento" uses lines from Ai, Robert Creeley, H. D., Lynn Emanuel, Carolyn Forché, Louise Glück, Mary Oliver, Adrienne Rich, and Tomas Tranströmer (translated by Samuel Charters and Robin Fulton).

"Evolution Cento" uses lines from Lucie Brock-Broido, H. D., Jorie Graham, Sara Eliza Johnson, Sharon Olds, Mary Oliver, Mary Ruefle, Tomas Tranströmer (translated by Robert Bly), and Jean Valentine.

"Haptic Cento" uses lines from Rae Armantrout, Michael Burkard, Leila Chatti, Donika Kelly, Alicia Ostriker, Carl Phillips, Jean Valentine, and William Carlos Williams.

"Nowhere Cento" uses lines from Ai, Michael Burkard, Lynn Emanuel, Mary Oliver, Sylvia Plath, and Tomas Tranströmer (translated by John F. Deane and May Swenson).

"Sorry Cento" uses lines from Michael Burkard, Robert Creeley, Louise Glück, Octavio Paz (translated by Muriel Rukeyser), Alejandra Pizarnik (translated by Yvette Siegert), Adrienne Rich, and Tomas Tranströmer (translated by Samuel Charters).

"Red Cento" uses lines from Michael Burkard, Louise Glück, Sara Eliza Johnson, Keith Leonard, Romeo Oriogun, and Mary Ruefle.

"Isolation Cento" uses lines from Robert Creeley, Carolyn Forché, H. D., Donika Kelly, Dorothea Lasky, Adrienne Rich, Mary Ruefle, William Carlos Williams, and Jane Wong.

"Epistolary Cento" uses lines from Ai, Michael Burkard, Robert Creeley, H. D., Lynn Emanuel, Louise Glück, Jorie Graham, Carolyn Forché, Vievee Francis, Sara Eliza Johnson, Sharon Olds, Mary Oliver, Alejandra Pizarnik (translated by Yvette Siegert), Sylvia Plath, Tomas Tranströmer (translated by Gunnar Harding, Frederic Will, and Robin Fulton), and Jean Valentine.

ACKNOWLEDGMENTS

So many people contributed to the creation of this book. Thank you to Patricia Smith for believing in these poems, and to D. S. Cunningham, Janet Foxman, Charlie Shields, and everyone at the University of Arkansas Press. Special thanks to Kwame Dawes and Hope Wabuke, who were instrumental in their guidance, support, and thoughtful insights as this book took shape. Thank you to Stacey Waite—my teacher forever. And thank you to Ted Kooser, Grace Bauer, and the many other teachers at the University of Nebraska-Lincoln and elsewhere who have inspired and influenced me.

I am so grateful to the community I've found in Lincoln: thank you, in partic-ular, to Saddiq Dzukogi, who was the first to read many of these poems and who supported the writing of this book more than anyone. Thanks to Katie Marya for her friendship and editorial eye. Thanks to Ilana Masad for movie nights and smoke breaks and conversations about heartbreak. Thank you, Jamaica, Isaac, Ava, Jordan, Teo, Kate, Nicole, Erika, Jason, Charlotte, and Tryphena. There are many, many others; I am grateful to you all.

Thank you to my cohort and community at Syracuse University, especially Erin (my ride or die), Lindsay, Anastasia, Emma, Becca, Jessica, Grady, and Chen. Thanks to Michael Burkard, Christopher Kennedy, and Bruce Smith for their guidance early in my writing life. Thank you to Sarah Harwell for being a force of kindness.

Thank you, Katee. You have showed me what friendship is and can be. You are an incredible human, mother, and friend.

This book is dedicated to the farms I've been fortunate enough to work on and the people and families who have welcomed me there. Thank you to the Olivers, who opened the door for all of this. Thank you to the Mathers, who brought horses into my life and these poems. Thank you to Suzy and Taylor at In Season and to the Shadowbrook team: Ian, Laura, Francisco, Diana, Salley, Kevin, and Charuth.

Finally, I am forever grateful for my family, especially my mother, who helped shape the artist in me and encouraged a life led by and devoted to creativity. This book, this life, would not have happened without you.

Many thanks to the following publications and other outlets where these poems first appeared: *Adirondack Review* ("PA-184 toward Steam Valley"); *Adroit Journal* ("Balm"); *Autofocus Lit* ("Aubade with Resurrection" and "Picking

Mulberries"); *Best New Poets* ("Milkstone"); *BOAAT Journal* ("Sorry Cento"); *Cortland Review* ("Hunter's Moon"); *Cotton Xenomorph* ("Greenbrier"); *Fairy Tale Review* ("Evolution Cento," "Firelight Cento," "Forest Cento," and "Ghazal for an Imagined Future"); *Figure 1* ("In the Forest of Dreams Left Scavenging"); *Half Mystic* ("On Desire"); *Hobart* ("Isolation Cento"); *Hot Metal Bridge* ("Red Ocher"); *IDK Magazine* ("Poem for When You Realize That You'll Never Look at Brussels Sprouts the Same Way Again" and "Unrequited Love Poem"); *Juked* ("3 A.M. Cento," "Aubade with Benediction," "Chores," and "When the Horse Lies Down"); *Meridian* ("Prothalamion"); *New Ohio Review* ("Mukahara"); *Poet Lore* ("Nowhere Cento"); Poets.org, "2020 University and College Poetry Prize Winners" ("Holmes Lake"); *Redivider* ("Ode to Seventh-Grade Girls"); *Rogue Agent* ("Haptic Cento"); *Salamander* ("Gastronomy"); *The Shore* ("Archival" and "To My First Lover"); *Sixth Finch* ("How to Change"); *South Carolina Review* ("Pennsylvania Backwoods Elegy"); *Southern Indiana Review* ("Knowledge"); *Timber* ("Epistolary Cento"); and *West Review* ("The Morning After"). "PA-184 toward Steam Valley" and "We've Been Saying Goodbye All Morning" previously appeared in the chapbook *Glassland* (JMWW, 2014). "The Barn" previously appeared in the chapbook *The Egg Mistress* (Gold Line Press, 2013).